POOL

POOL

Mike Shamos

MALLARD PRESS

MALLARD PRESS
An imprint of BDD Promotional Book Company, Inc.
666 Fifth Avenue
New York, New York 10103

A TERN ENTERPRISE BOOK
Published by MALLARD PRESS
An imprint of BDD Promotional Book Company, Inc.
666 Fifth Avenue
New York, New York 10103

Mallard Press and its accompanying design and logo are trademarks
of BDD Promotional Book Company, Inc.

ISBN 0-7924-5310-7

POOL
was prepared and produced by
Tern Enterprise Inc.
15 West 26th Street
New York, New York 10010

Designer: Kingsley Parker
Photo Editor: Ede Rothaus
Illustrations by Helayne Messing

Picture Credits and Acknowledgements:

pp. 8, 10, 11, 13, 16, 17a, 17b, 18a, 18b, 19, 20a, 20b, 21, 22, 23,
24, 25, 26, 27a, 27b, 28, 29a, 29b, 30, 31a, 31b, 31c, 32a, 32b, 33a,
33b, 36a, 36b, 37, 38a, 38b, 39, 40, 41, 42, 44, 45, 46, 48, 54, 59,
60, 63a, 63b, 65a, 65b, 66, 67, 68, 70, 75b, 76, 77, 78, 81, 82a, 84,
85, 86, 89, 92, 93, 94a, 94b, 98, 99, 100a, 100b, 101, 102, 106,
107a, 108b, 109, 110a, 110b, 114a, 114b, 115, 117, 122, 123
The Billiard Archive

pp. 51, 56 Allsport; p. 111 Courtesy of Billiards Digest; p. 108 © Billie
Billing; pp. 72, 74, 75 Courtesy of Blatt Billiards, New York; pp. 28,
29, 56a, 82b, 90a, 96, 100 © Jeff Greenberg; pp. 50a, 50b, 52, 87a,
87b, 90b, 91, 96, 103, 105 © David Leah/Allsport; p. 107 © Carmine
Manicone; pp. 56b, 58, 119, 121b © Bob Martin/Allsport; pp. 14, 34,
104 © Don Rogers/Instock; pp. 118, 121a © Pascal Rondeau/Allsport;
pp. 112, 116, 120 Bob Thomas Sports Photography;

Typeset by Bookworks Plus
Color separation by Excel Graphic Arts Co.
Printed and bound in Hong Kong by LeeFung-Asco Printers Ltd.

DEDICATION

To my children, Josselyn and Alexander.
With daddy's love.

I have been dreaming for years about a book that would tell the inside story of pool in an entertaining and visual way. Stephen Williams, of Tern Enterprise, provided me with the opportunity to produce one, but I have many people to thank for the trip that led to this volume:

My father, Morris Shamos, who took me into a billiard parlor when I was in high school and showed me how to make a draw shot. He has been wondering about the wisdom of that action ever since.

My mother, Marion, who tried in vain to discourage me from frequenting pool halls. Had she been successful, these pages would be blank.

My wife, Julie, who was brave enough to sit in McGirr's poolroom in the 1960s to watch me play. Those of you who saw the place know the depth of her sacrifice.

A security guard at Princeton University, whose name I forgot long ago, who introduced me to three-cushions in 1964. I am sure he had no idea what this innocent favor would lead to.

Dan O'Leary, who taught me the techniques of hustling through a series of expensive but unforgettable lessons. Dan now enjoys a respectable career outside billiards, so I won't give out any other information that might reveal where he lives.

Frank Masland IV, my playing partner in college, who showed me a lot about straight pool and handicapping techniques. He now enjoys a respectable career *inside* billiards.

Thanks are also due to Mike Panozzo, the editor of *Billiards Digest,* for providing me with access to his magazine's extensive historical records and photographs, as well as offering me the chance to publish a regular column on billiard history; Bob Byrne, the premier instructional writer on the game, who has encouraged my historical work and supplied me with many items and insights; Ed Elgin, manager of Cue & Cushion in Springfield, Illinois, which was named 1947's "Room of the Future," provided photographs of his remarkable facility as well as his views on the game in the postwar period; the Hillman Library of the University of Pittsburgh, which allowed me unlimited use of its microform collection.

Finally, I want to recognize the contribution of the Billiard Archive, an unsung, nonprofit historical organization in Pittsburgh that strives to preserve, study, and maintain the history of billiards by acquiring and caring for antique books, prints, photographs, and other artifacts of the game. I am privileged to serve as its curator. All of the prints and photographs reproduced in this book are from the archive's collection. If you are interested in its work and mission, please give us a call at (412) 681–8916.

My debts are many—my tributes inadequate.

Mike Shamos
Pittsburgh, Pennsylvania

ALBERT FREY.
ALLEN & GINTER'S
RICHMOND. Cigarettes. VIRGINIA.

J. L. MALONE.
ALLEN & GINTER'S
RICHMOND. Cigarettes. VIRGINIA.

CONTENTS

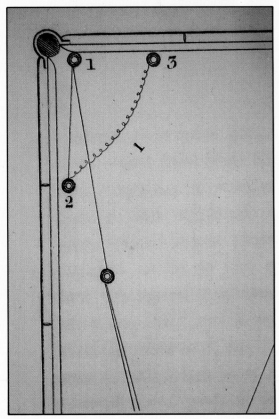

INTRODUCTION

Put simply, billiards is a game in which balls are pushed around on a table with wooden sticks. Pool is the same except that the table has pockets. That's all there is to it—balls, sticks, pockets, the tools of one of the most riveting human diversions. Why is billiards so fascinating? For one thing, when you pick up a cue, you are sharing an experience enjoyed by Louis XIV, Mark Twain, Marie Antoinette, Mozart, George Washington, Napoleon, Charles Dickens, Abraham Lincoln, W.C. Fields, Queen Victoria, and Babe Ruth, to name a few of the most notable players. The game is also popular among the Mafia, white-collar criminals, drug kingpins, and stockbrokers, as well as bums, loiterers, hustlers, and lunatics. (Pool tables have been used for therapeutic purposes in asylums for over 150 years.) But perhaps most intriguing, billiard parlors (or "pool rooms") have long been thought to attract people who make a living by their wits and talent rather than by conventional employment. There is always something appealing about feats of manual dexterity like juggling, legerdemain, and pool shooting. A player who can make the balls work magic will always have an audience.

Why do so many people love playing billiards? It's simple really. The game isn't strenuous—you don't need to be an athlete, and you can play from childhood literally until death. (Several famous players have died at the table; others have committed suicide after losing important matches.) The rules are easy to understand. You don't need expensive equipment. You can play at home alone or with as large a group as will fit around the table. You can eat, drink, smoke, talk, and gamble during the game. The balls even make a nice clicking noise when they hit each other and drop into pockets. You can wear casual clothes, formal attire, or nothing at all. You can play in private clubs, student centers, posh nightclubs,

Au Café, *an oil painting by Paul Gaugin, 1888. Vincent Van Gogh and Gaugin were friends. This is the same cafe that was painted by Van Gogh in* The Night Cafe *(see page 22).*

The Pennsylvania State Lunatic Hospital, c. 1880. Pool has been offered as a recreation in asylums for about 150 years. Alas, more people have been driven crazy by pool during that time than have been cured by it.

grimy pool halls, and on military installations, either day or night. It is a game of skill at which you can watch your level of performance steadily increase. To quote the Music Man's song *Ya Got Trouble*, it develops a "cool hand and a keen eye." There are many variations and fine gradations of handicapping to equalize the abilities of different players. You can watch it on television and attend or enter tournaments. In short, it is a game for all people in all places and at all times.

Today, billiards is experiencing its greatest revival in five hundred years. After a long period of dormancy, the game has become chic and upscale. Modern rooms offer "yuppie pool" (which seems to mean you can drink Perrier at the table). Some people pay more for a fancy cue stick now than they do for a whole table. Movies, music videos, and television shows are likely to depict contemporary

lifestyles by showing people playing pool. The new poolrooms are social centers where you are as likely to meet your spouse as you are to learn how to pocket a ball. Women are enjoying the game in unparalleled numbers.

A Few Terms

To get the ball rolling, so to speak, here's a quick course in terminology. *Billiards* is often used generically to mean any game played on a billiard table, whether or not pockets are present.

Pool means any billiard game in which there are pockets on the table, such as straight pool, nine-ball, and eight-ball. When a player says, "Let's shoot some pool," this could mean any of these games or more than two hundred others. The usual object in pool is to strike the white ball, known as the "cue ball," with your cue stick, make the cue ball hit another ball, called an "object ball," and cause the object ball to enter a pocket.

Billiards is also used in contrast to pool to refer to any game in which there are no pockets on the table and only three or four balls are used, the goal being to make a *carom*, in which you force the cue ball to hit at least two of the other balls. In this book, I will use *carom billiards* to indicate this form of billiards and distinguish it from the more generic *billiards*. The most popular form of carom billiards in the United States is *three-cushion* billiards, a sublime game in which you must cause your cue ball to make three cushion contacts before completing a carom.

The Heyday

Billiards may have been born in Europe, but it flourished in America beyond all expectations. In 1800 there were hardly a dozen public tables in New York. By the 1830s the game had spread throughout the city. The first important public room was Bassford's, at 630 Broadway, featuring twenty tables and a clientele composed mainly of stockbrokers and professional men.

The driving force behind billiards in the United States was Michael Phelan, an Irish immigrant who at age thirty-three wrote the first American book devoted to the game. His *Billiards Without a Master*, published in 1850 and now very rare, introduced several important innovations, including diamonds, small markers attached to the rails to assist with aiming.

During the 1850s, interest in billiards increased to the point that public competitions were held for paying spectators. In 1858, the New York Times began reporting the results of matches. The following year, thousands of people filled Fireman's Hall in Detroit to see Phelan himself beat John Seereiter for the astronomical prize of fifteen thousand dollars (by contrast, the first prize in the U.S. Open Pocket Billiard Tournament held 130 years later was only ten thousand dollars). Phelan, an accomplished inventor and businessman as well as a player, used his winnings to form a table manufacturing company. Through a series of mergers, it became Phelan and Collender, then joined with J.M. Brunswick and Balke to form the Brunswick-Balke-Collender Company, whose successor is today's Brunswick Corporation, the largest American manufacturer of billiard tables.

Over the next twenty years, billiard competitions attracted great crowds and front-page newspaper treatment. This was at a time when leading newspapers were no more than eight pages long and sometimes two columns were devoted to a billiard match while Civil War events merited only one. Attendance by women was always mentioned in the coverage; sometimes women were admitted free (when accompanied by gentlemen) in an effort to raise the level of gentility. Gambling was legal, and bettors shouted out changing odds during the game. This kept audience interest at a fever pitch but did little to help the popular image of the game.

The term *poolroom* acquired its negative connotation during this period, largely due to a linguistic misunderstanding. The invention of the telegraph allowed the results of horse races to be sent across the country instantaneously and inspired offtrack betting. Racing fans assembled in rooms to place their bets, which were "pooled" to determine the odds. Thus, these establishments became known as poolrooms. Delays between races were long, so the rooms provided billiard tables to alleviate boredom. *Pool* was also the name of one of the billiard games of the day, and an indelible association between billiard parlors and poolrooms was formed in the public mind.

Another equipment development

Michael Phelan (1817–1871) Born in Ireland, Phelan was a player, author, columnist, and table manufacturer who can be considered the father of American billiards. His 1850 treatise, *Billiards Without a Master*, was the first book on the game published in the United States. This was followed in 1857 by *The Game of Billiards*, which appeared in at least eleven editions. In 1859, Phelan beat John Seereiter at a match in Detroit for the astounding sum of fifteen thousand dollars, which he used to form a table-manufacturing company that evolved through several mergers into the current Brunswick Corporation. Holder of many billiard patents, Phelan was probably the first to set markers into the table rails to assist in aiming.

The great billiard tournament, at Irving Hall, New York, April 27, 1869. The Match Between William Goldthwait and Edward Daniels, *a wood engraving from* Leslie's, *May 15, 1869. The game is American four-ball billiards on a four-pocket table. The players' representatives and the scorekeeper are seated at the left. Note the preponderance of men in the audience.

marked the next turning point in the game. Billiard balls were made of ivory, which was expensive because a single elephant tusk yielded only three or four balls, so incredible ingenuity was directed at the problem of developing a substitute. Metal balls were tried, along with various compositions, including strips of cloth dipped in shellac and formed into a spherical shape. Nothing was really effective until John Wesley Hyatt invented celluloid in 1868. Despite the fact that his balls would occasionally explode, Hyatt's innovation made him wealthy. The holder of 235 patents, he formed the Albany Billiard Ball Company and revolutionized the industry.

For the remainder of the nineteenth century, the challenge for the billiard industry was to develop just the right competitive formula for the game to satisfy increasing legions of fans. During this period, players became so expert at making caroms that their play became boring to an extreme. Long runs were made by grazing the cue ball against two other balls, moving them only a fraction of an inch. The audience could neither see nor hear the motion and had to be content with listening to the referee drone on counting points. A game had to be devised that would force players to make visible shots.

Beginning in 1879, lines known as "balklines" were drawn with chalk on the cloth of the table to divide its surface into different areas. Various restrictions were imposed requiring shooters to knock balls into or out of these regions or lose their turns. No matter what constraints were devised, however, players developed skills to overcome them. Professional players practiced minute variations on a shot for hours each day, ready to unleash a new tactic at the next tournament. This was before the rise of organized team sports in America. Billiard players were the celebrities of the sporting scene, more important than champion boxers. Their habits and prospects were analyzed incessantly in print, along with speculation on the odds to be offered at their next appearance.

Starting around 1900, world tournaments were established in pocket, balkline, and three-cushion billiards. These events produced genuine stars, who not only visited billiard rooms to give exhibitions, but were frequent vaudeville performers, sandwiching a trickshot demonstration in between a dog act and a comedy troupe.

By 1925, the *New York Times* carried not one, but several, articles per day about billiards. The game was used to promote all kinds of products and figured in many publicity stunts. Willie Hoppe, who won a world tournament at age eighteen, rode around Chicago playing billiards on top of a Studebaker.

It may surprise you, but based on newspaper and magazine articles of the day, as well as the number of billiard licenses issued and tables sold, it appears that billiards was the chief sport for men in the United States from the 1850s until the 1930s.

Modern Billiards

After the stock market crash of 1929, the American public began to lose interest in billiards. During the 1930s it was difficult for any business to survive. At the start of the depression, there were over five thousand public billiard rooms in Manhattan. Billiard establishments, which were usually small, closed in great numbers. The gaiety of the 1920s also gave way to a more somber attitude toward pool. The game was declared sinful by preachers and politicians alike, and restrictive legislation was passed all over the country. New York State forbade the use of the word *pool* in connection with a billiard room, as though changing the name alone could improve the character of the game. In fact, remnants of this period still survive in municipal ordinances: New York does not permit alcohol to be served in billiard rooms; some towns in Iowa require their rooms to close at 9 P.M. and in San Francisco minors are allowed to play, but only if they can be seen by a police car passing in the street!

The Brunswick Corporation tried everything to keep interest in the game alive, including such fanciful innovations as yellow balls and purple cloth on the tables and telegraphic tournaments, in which players could communicate shots by wire to avoid the need to travel to tournaments and play in person.

In the end, it was World War II that was responsible for reviving the game—at least for a while. Virtually every military installation had pool tables. The famous

Cyrille Dion (1834–1878) Born in Montreal, this left-handed player was known as the "Bismarck of Billiards." He was a champion of Canada and won the last American four-ball championship in 1873. Soon after three-ball billiards competitions began, Dion won the world championship in 1875. Turning to pool, he won the first tournament for the Championship of America title in April 1878. His spectacular career was sadly cut short when he died fewer than six months later, still champion, at the age of thirty-five. Dion's two brothers were also players. One of them, Joseph, was a world titleholder, but went insane and spent decades in asylums, supported by contributions from his fellow billiards players.

Ralph Greenleaf and his wife, Princess Nai-Tai-Tai, Detroit, December 16, 1929 (this page). Greenleaf was in town for the world pocket billiards championship tournament. He was persuaded to try shooting pool in an airplane as a publicity stunt, using a five-foot-long table. That evening he set a new high run record of 126 in his match against Frank Taberski. (The 1927 date written on the image is incorrect.) The Cue & Cushion (opposite page), known as the "room of the future," opened in Springfield, Illinois in 1947.

Designed to prove that billiards could be played in wholesome surroundings, the room featured a soda fountain, lessons, and pool leagues. The Springfield Women's Club found the place so respectable that they met there for lunch every Tuesday. The Cue & Cushion sported only the best Brunswick equipment, some of which was created just for this facility. While it succeeded in upgrading the image of pool, the room was not a commercial success and closed after fifteen months. The room anticipated the upscale parlors of the 1990s by forty years.

players of the day, most of whom were in the service themselves, gave countless exhibitions for the troops. Even stars who were too old to enlist, such as Willie Hoppe and Charles C. Peterson, a great trick-shot artist, traveled extensively for the military.

Tournaments flourished with early-twentieth-century stars Ralph Greenleaf and Willie Hoppe still active, joined by such emerging champions as Jimmy Caras, Willie Mosconi, and Irving Crane. But when the war ended in 1945, the returning veterans were much more concerned with responsible pursuits, such as finding jobs and housing, than with pool, and once again the game declined.

Urban troubles were ultimately the most effective enemy of the billiard parlor. Ames Billiards, the Times Square fixture used in the filming of *The Hustler*, fell victim to New York Mayor Lindsay's cleanup of that area in the mid-1960s. Detroit Recreation, the largest poolroom in the country with well over one hundred tables, and Allinger's in Philadelphia, the scene of many world tournaments, closed unceremoniously. McGirr's, a famous basement room on Eighth Avenue in New York which sponsored Willie Mosconi in the 1940s, fell thirty years later when police wiretaps disclosed that drug deals were being arranged there. The last of the great emporiums, Palace Billiards in San Francisco lost its lease in 1988, when the building that housed it became too valuable to tolerate a poolroom.

For the next fifteen to twenty years, pool was able to survive only through home play and eight-ball pool leagues, which use tables two feet shorter than the standard size. Fans without tables would have had trouble locating a public poolroom even if they had wanted one. As a consequence of this drought, nearly a generation of technical billiard knowledge was lost. This is not to deny that there are thousands of expert players around, but skill is passed on by experts working with students over a long period of time. On the other hand, the lengthy lull appears to have had a powerful cleansing effect on the game. Nearly all the old style parlors have closed, hustling has virtually disappeared, and many young people have no notion of the way pool used to be. The result: loss of stigma.

These days people who would never have stepped inside a classic poolroom see pool as chic. The change in the game's status has been credited to *The Color of Money*, a sequel to *The Hustler*, released a quarter-century later, in 1986. Paul Newman, who played Fast Eddie Felson in both films, received an Oscar for *The Color of Money* and a Best Actor nomination for *The Hustler*. But it was the character played by Tom Cruise—a talented, cocky, but naive young player who learns the fine art of hustling from Felson—that showed a new generation that pool could be wild and fun, as well as profitable.

While movies have shown an ability to start trends, they rarely sustain them.

As the old rooms were closing, however, the 1961 release of the movie *The Hustler* created a short-lived pool boom. Just seeing Jackie Gleason with a cue in his hand made people itch to get to the table. New establishments opened around the country to satisfy popular demand. But few lasted. The sixties were full of energy and rebellion. There was scant interest in a somewhat disreputable, languid activity practiced in smoke-filled male environments. By the start of the seventies, billiards was in the deepest slump it had experienced literally in centuries.

That takes real money, not just the color of it. More than anything else, it is the changing economics of the game that have built a new foundation for the billiards industry. Until recently, the vast majority of billiards establishments in the United States have been family owned and lacking in the capital necessary to outlast the slump.

Why is a poolroom a viable business? The cost of a pool table has not increased (if you consider inflation) since 1860. But the rate that can be charged for table time has gone up by a factor of four in as many years. This means that any investment in billiard equipment can be earned back with startling speed. The calculation is easy. Assuming a table price tag of $2,500 and a rate of $10 per hour, the cost can be amortized in 250 hours of play. Even if the table is used only eight hours per day, the outlay is recovered in about a month!

Modern rooms offer attractive decor, refreshments, and exhibit no tolerance

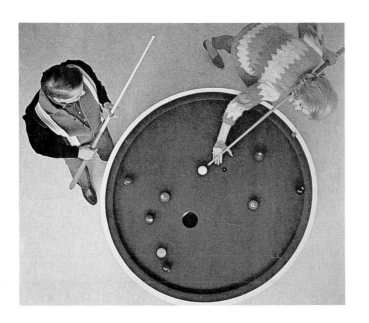

for loitering or hustlers preying on customers. Many offer lessons and sell a range of equipment including books and instructional videotapes. They attract an upscale clientele that plays for recreation, not for lack of anything better to do.

The new popularity of pool has spread quickly to Boston, Atlanta, Chicago, Florida, and Los Angeles. The game is everywhere now, in product endorsements and on prime-time television. And for the first time women are joining the ranks of pool players by the thousands—a sure sign that pool is back!

Circular pool table (left) *with one off-center pocket. This game variation was tried in the 1960s but never achieved popularity. The standard continues to be the rectangular pool table* (opposite, and above).

Women in Billiards

Ruth McGinnis (1910–1974) The left-handed "Queen of Billiards" began playing pool at age seven in her father's room. By eleven, she had run 25 and at fourteen she defeated the Flower sisters, then the world champions in women's billiards. She was the women's world champion from 1932 to 1940.

In a series of 1,532 exhibition games, she only lost 29 over a seven-year period. One of her victims was Babe Didrikson, one of America's foremost women of sport. McGinnis's exhibition high run at straight pool was 128; she once ran 125 in tournament play. During the 1940s she was invited to play in men's competition, including the United States national tournament. Despite her fame as a billiard player, McGinnis was devoted to her lifelong career of teaching retarded children.

Contrary to popular opinion, women have played billiards since its very inception. The first published reference to the game, which appeared in the *Journal de Paris*, mentions a seductive woman named Margot, who was able to beat any man. In fact, it's such an early article that it is not even clear whether it refers to ground billiards or the table version. Through the years, a number of royal women enjoyed the game. Mary, Queen of Scots lamented being kept from billiards during her imprisonment in 1576, and in a gruesome but fitting tribute to her pastime, her body was wrapped in the cloth from her table after her execution.

Generally speaking, the mixing of the sexes over a billiard table in public houses was frowned upon during the early days of the game. In 1716, the electors of Saxony enacted an ordinance stating that only men could work in billiard rooms. But the most insulting evidence of discrimination during the eighteenth century concerned the use of the cue—only men were allowed to shoot with it, out of fear that women would tear the cloth due to inferior skill. Women were forced to use the mace instead, a custom that was justified by the fact that they could do so without having to bend over and thus expose their underskirts. Women were not depicted using the cue in any illustrations for almost fifty years after its invention, until the early nineteenth century.

Nobles could do as they pleased, however, which is one of the benefits of rank. Marie Antoinette owned a cue made of a single piece of ivory. She reportedly valued it so much that she wore the key to the cabinet in which it was stored around her neck. Napoleon and Josephine were also enthusiastic players. He was fond of *finger billiards*, a bizarre game in which the balls are shot with the hand, a method that allows extreme spin to be applied. But the fact remains that billiards has always been confined largely to male enclaves—social clubs, saloons, and poolrooms. In the past women who wanted to play faced huge obstacles, including being taunted by both men and other women, as though they were prostitutes.

Despite the relatively small number of women players, there is no shortage of historical artwork portraying them. However, they are never shown displaying sound technique. The vast majority of illustrations show them sitting on the table or shooting behind their back which gave the men a chance to admire a prominent bosom. Even Alice Howard, a female exhibition player and author of two books on pool, claimed in a talk in 1919: "A billiard table shows a woman off to advantage. How could a fetching ankle be better displayed than when dangling from a billiard table as the owner of the ankle balances herself on the edge of the table for a shot?"

Napoleon at billiards (left), *from a painting by Clinedienst. The lady is not Josephine, but the Emperor's consort, Maria Louisa of Austria. At left is Field Marshal Ney. Napoleon was an enthusiastic player who had a billiard table during his exile on St. Helena. Pretty petticoat pool players. The passion which has been recently developed among New York damsels—their proficiency as witnessed in the back-room of a bier saloon* (below, left), *a wood engraving from the* National Police Gazette, *April 16, 1881.* Jessie Remained Alone at the Table, *by Winslow Homer* (left), *a wood engraving that appeared in* The Gallery, *July, 1867. Though he was later to become a celebrated American painter, Homer produced this print while he was still a journeyman newspaper illustrator. When played in the proper surroundings, billiards was regarded as a polite accomplishment for ladies.*

Untitled lithograph by Maurice Neumon, 1905 (left). Carom billiards in an exquisite setting. Private clubs kept the game respectable when public rooms were socially unacceptable. Billiards, an etching by Anders Zorn, 1898 (right). This image scandalized the Paris art world because it showed Zorn's mistress playing caroms alone, with her bosom exposed. This etching is one of the few prints of the era that showed a woman using good billiard techniques.

La Partie de Billard [The Billiard Party], *by R. Prinet, c. 1900 (right). Women would often shoot behind their backs in order to reach shots conveniently. An uncouth commentator suggested that the pose showed off their figures to advantage.*

Some billiard sources actually debated whether women had the physical and mental capability to play billiards, and some proposed to ban them entirely from the game on the grounds that their senses were too delicate to survive the filth of a pool hall. It was even suggested as early as 1900 that the female arm was anatomically incapable of developing a good stroke! Of course, it is obvious that, in fact, women have not been welcomed into the billiard community in the past except as curiosities, have not had role models or mentors to learn from, and have not enjoyed any moral support or reward for success. Those who succeeded possessed exceptional fortitude.

It has become fashionable to point to such unusual players as Ruth McGinnis, a star in the thirties and forties who had a high run—a series of consecutive points made in a single turn at a table—in straight pool of 128; Masako Katsura, a Japanese woman who entered the World Three-Cushion Tournament three times; Dorothy Wise, a grandmother who won the first five U.S. Open Pocket Billiard titles; and Jean Balukas, who played in her first U.S. Open at age nine, won the title on seven occasions, and was the first woman to run over 130, as proof that sex is no barrier to billiards skill. But these women were exceptions in their time.

The present rebirth of pool has produced a large contingent of female players. Among the current top competitors are Ewa (pronounced "Eva") Mataya, Loree Jon Jones, and Robin Bell. Mataya is a former model who holds the U.S. Open Straight-Pool high run of 54 and is an insightful television commentator; Jones is a businesswoman who has won national straight-pool and nine-ball titles; Bell is a mother of five who took the 1990 World Pool-Billiard Association Nine-Ball crown in West Germany. A number of the newer poolrooms have women instructors, and the Women's Professional Billiard Association (WPBA) is assuring a steady supply of women's tournaments and increasing prize money.

Finally, it is no longer awkward for women to patronize a billiard parlor, any more than it would be for them to go bowling or play tennis. No one—other than some crusty (male) sportswriters—has cause to bemoan the disappearance of smoky poolrooms and the rise of women's billiards.

Jean Balukas (1959–) Balukas is a certified phenomenon. Having learned the game at her family's poolroom in Brooklyn she entered the United States open straight pool tournament at age nine and finished fifth. She won the event seven consecutive times beginning in 1972, stopping only when competition was disbanded. Balukas is probably the strongest women's player ever. Her unofficial high run exceeds 150 balls, higher than McGinnis's 128, and as of 1989 she had won more tournament money than any other woman. Proficient at baseball, basketball, and tennis as well as pool, in 1985 Balukas became the youngest player to join the BCA Hall of Fame.

2

GAMES

A prodigious number of different games can be played on a billiard table. Over three hundred have been described in print, and variations number in the thousands. Out of this collection of amusements, only about ten are played regularly in the United States, and only three can be said to be truly popular: nine-ball, eight-ball, and straight pool. One-pocket, three-cushion billiards, and snooker are also seen; bank pool and rotation are somewhat less popular. There are other games that have only regional appeal.

In England, snooker is the overwhelming favorite, with eight-ball advancing in popularity. A hardy few still play English billiards, described later in this chapter.

While snooker is played all over the world, a handful of games never seen in the United States or England are common in other countries. *Pin billiards*, or *casín* (pronounced "ka-SEEN"), is the choice in Latin American countries and Italy. It is played with three balls and five small wooden pins that are placed near the center of the table. The object is to hit the cue ball into one of the other two and cause that ball to knock down one or more pins. In the Orient, a version of carom billiards is played using four balls (two whites and two reds). The idea is to make a carom on the reds without hitting the other white.

It would be far beyond the scope of this book to include the rules for all these games. For that, you will need the *Official Rule Book*, available from the Billiard Congress of America. Instead, this chapter provides some insight into the most commonly played games, including their origins.

The patriarch of all modern billiard games is a seventeenth-century game called simply "billiards." In those days the game was played with only two balls on a table with six pockets, or, occasionally, no pockets. Sometimes a hoop known as a

The point of origin for all modern billiard games was a seventeenth-century game that was played with only two balls on a table that had six pockets or, occasionally, on a table with no pockets. Variations on the possible games that can be played on a billiard table number in the thousands.

Carom Billiards and Balkline

Straight-rail billiards is just the old game of French caroms. The last professional tournament was held in 1879, but the game is still played by amateurs even today. The reason it died as a professional test is that players became so expert at it they virtually never missed. Not only would a player remain at the table for hours, but the motion of the balls was so minute that spectators could see nothing. When Jacob Schaefer, Sr., ran 690 points in 1879, the game was literally up.

During the 1880s, lines known as "balklines" were drawn on the table with chalk to divide it into rectangular areas. The rule was that when both object balls were lying in one rectangle, a player could make only a very small number of points, usually just 1 or 2, before he was forced to make at least one of the balls leave the box.

The first balkline game used lines drawn eight inches from the cushions. This was soon increased to ten inches, then twelve, fourteen, and, by 1896, to eighteen inches. Balkline games were identified by numbers that indicated the distance of the lines from the cushions and the number of shots allowed before a ball had to be driven out. For example, 18.1 balkline is played with eighteen-inch lines, one shot permitted with both balls in the same rectangle. In 1906, eighteen-year-old Willie Hoppe beat Maurice Vignaux of France for the world 18.1 title in Paris.

Most American billiard players today have never seen a game of balkline. Its popularity peaked during the 1920s and then rapidly faded in the thirties as three-cushions rose in prominence. Balkline is an incredibly exacting game that demands great patience and delicate, controlled stroke. It is still played in Europe, where metric measurements are used to number the games. A game called 47.2 balkline (meaning the lines are 47.2 centimeters, or about eighteen inches, from the cushions) is the most popular version.

Three-Cushion Billiards

Most people think of three-cushions as the most arcane billiard game of them all, played only by mathematical geniuses who have a supernatural command of angles and spin. The first time they see it many people have trouble just figuring out what the object is. Still, it is by far the most popular carom game in the United States today.

Three-cushion billiards evolved from carom billiards at about the same time as balkline and quickly became a favorite because of the game's spectacular shots and the extreme english needed to make them.

The rules are simple. It is played using the same equipment as straight-rail. In order to score a point, the cue ball must contact both object balls in either order but must make three distinct cushion impacts (not necessarily on different cushions) before hitting the second ball

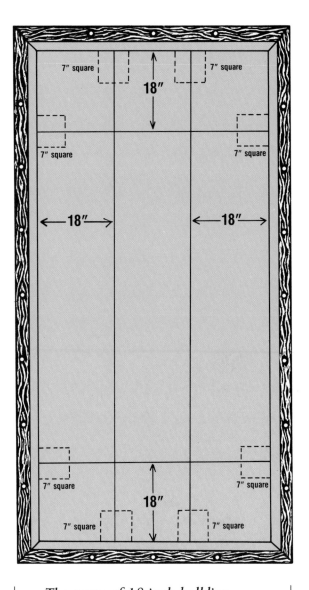

The game of 18-inch balkline. The lines are drawn with tailor's chalk. When both object balls lie within one of the eight boxes adjacent to the cushions, the player must make at least one of them leave the box within a predetermined number of shots. This highest expression of the billiard art died in the United States in the 1930s, but is still played in Europe and Japan.

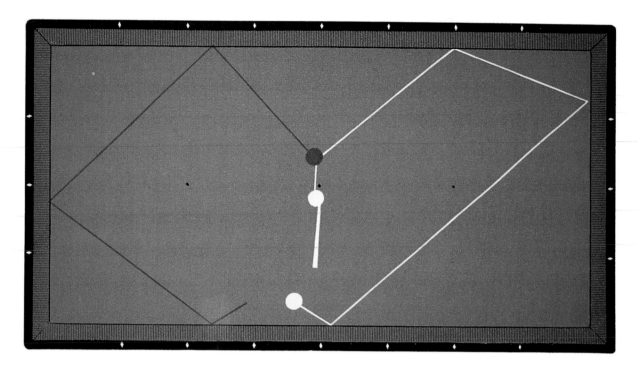

A typical three-cushion shot. The cue ball (taking the white path) must make three cushion contacts before completing the carom. Either object ball may be hit first and the contacts need not involve three different cushions. The diagram is from Scientific Billiards, *by Albert Garnier. Published in 1880, it was one of the first billiard books to have colored plates. Garnier won the first world championship at carom billiards, in New York in 1873.*

for the first time. That's all there is to it. Completing a shot according to the rules entitles the player to 1 point. Games are played to a fixed number of points, usually 50 in single games or sets of three 15-point games. Also, three-cushion is the only billiard game that guarantees "equal innings" to each player, in a fashion similar to baseball. If the player who scores the total number of points first was the opening breaker, his opponent is entitled to one more inning in which he may tie, but not win.

Three-cushion runs are rarely very high. A player who averages 1 point per inning is an extremely good player. The winner of the U.S. championship usually has an average between 0.900 and 1.100. The world tournament victor averages in the range 1.400 to 1.600. A run of 10 is impressive, a run of 15 stratospheric. If a player runs 20 he will be among only a handful who have ever done so and will

have matched the American competitive record. The world tournament record is 30, set by Yoshio Yoshihara of Japan in December 1988.

Three-cushion is unlike any other billiard or pool game. In many shots, the cue ball travels thirty feet or more and may keep moving for seven seconds. In pool, a ten-foot shot is a long one, and two seconds of motion is a lot. In three-cushions, an accurate, hard stroke is essential and english must be used just to get the ball to go around the table. Games are a real battle because neither player is likely to run out after an opponent's mistake. It is possible to win eleven consecutive games of nine-ball to win a match; that would be impossible in three-cushion, where no one has ever run out a 50-point game.

One of the most common reasons for missing a three-cushion shot is that the first object ball interferes with either the cue ball or the second object ball. Good players develop rules of thumb for deciding when such a "kiss" is likely to occur. More accurate calculations can be made using the diamond system, a method of predicting a ball's path as it moves around the table based on the small circular markers embedded in the rails. (They used to be a diamond shape, hence the name.) With the diamond system, the point at which the cue ball will contact the third cushion can be determined with great precision by means of simple subtraction. With some further work, the contact point on the fourth cushion can be worked out. The arithmetic required is elementary, and a simple illustration of this method can be seen in the 1959 Walt Disney cartoon *Donald in Mathmagic Land*, available on videotape.

Position play consists of making a shot and leaving the balls in locations from which another three-cushion shot can be made. This was long thought to be impossible. Even during the 1940s, when the game was at its height in the United States, players concentrated far more on defense than on trying for favorable offensive positions. Really advanced position players try for positions from which another *position* shot can be made. The prime consideration in position play is controlling where the first object ball will go, which is difficult because it usually travels far and is not struck directly with the cue stick. In some cases, it is even possible to take into account how the second object ball will be hit.

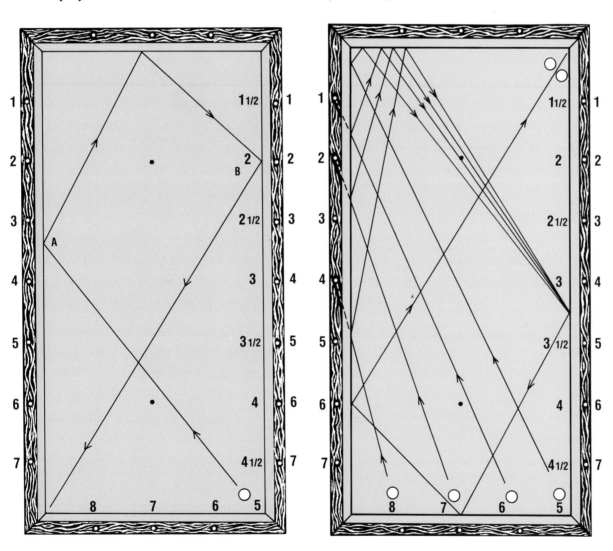

The diamond system. Numbers are assigned to the diamonds so that the path of the cue ball can be predicted by a simple mathematical calculation. At far left, a ball banked around the table from the corner into the third diamond on the long rail with a particular degree of spin will return directly into the other corner. At left, is a system for five-cushion bank shots. The diagrams are from System Play in Three-Cushion, *by E. H. Barry (1928), the first American book on the diamond system.*

Snooker

Snooker is a challenging hybrid of billiards played all over the world, but mostly in the United Kingdom and in areas formerly under British control, such as India and Singapore.

According to legend, snooker was developed around 1875, by a British officer in India who combined two popular games of the day, pyramid pool and black pool. In its modern form, snooker is played with a cue ball, fifteen red balls and six colored balls—yellow, green, brown, blue, pink, and black—called the "colours" (British spelling), or the "pool balls," reflecting the game's ancestry. These are slightly smaller than in American pool and have numerical values from two to seven in order from yellow to black; reds are each worth 1 point. The values are not marked on the balls as they are in the United States.

Snooker is played on an English billiards table measuring six by twelve feet, with narrow pockets. Pocketing balls, or "potting" as it is known in Britain, is very difficult, and there is tremendous emphasis on aiming and straight stroking. Little english is used, which is ironic in view of the origin of the term.

The opening striker shoots his cue ball from within the D-shaped area and must hit a red ball first. If he sinks one, he can then pick ("nominate") a colour and contact it first on his next stroke. If he sinks the nominated colour, it is returned to its spot and he must then hit a red again, and so forth, alternating between reds

and colours until he misses. So long as there are reds on the table, each player must contact one as his first shot on every turn. When only the cue ball and the six colours remain on the table, the colours must be contacted in numerical order, and remain off the table when they are pocketed. At any point, the ball that the player must contact next is called the "ball on." One rack of snooker is called a "frame" and is played until all the balls have been pocketed or one player concedes. The player having the most points when this occurs is the winner. Under certain conditions, a frame of snooker may end earlier.

Snooker is unique among billiard games in that a player can score both offensively—that is, by pocketing balls—and defensively, by making a legal shot but leaving the opponent in a position from which he fouls. The rules for scoring fouls are complicated, but are based on simple principles. All fouls by a player cause points to be *added* to his opponent's score, not deducted from his own. The usual fouls in other billiard games are also fouls in snooker, such as stroking without one foot on the floor, touching a ball, hitting a ball twice, and the like. It is also a foul to fail to hit the ball on. The cost of a foul varies from 4 points to 7 and is generally the value of the ball on or the ball contacted, whichever is higher. For example, if a player is on reds and fails to hit any ball at all, the penalty is 4 points, the minimum. If he is on reds but hits the pink first, the penalty is 6, the value of the pink. If he accidentally touches a red after nominating blue, the penalty is 5, the value of the ball on.

In English games, a run of points is called a "break," usage unrelated to the American "break shot." In snooker the maximum length of a break is 147 points, achieved by taking a red and the black fifteen times for 8 points each time, then by potting the colours in order, yielding a total of $(15 \times 8) + 2 + 3 + 4 + 5 + 6 + 7 = 147$. The first official maximum break in snooker was not recorded until 1948, and occurrences are much rarer than a run of 150 in straight pool.

Snooker was a minor game in England until 1969, when it was first televised regularly by the British Broadcasting Corporation. Steve Davis, now the top-ranked player, earns more in a single year than all United States professional pool players combined. A televised snooker match can be truly exciting when accompanied by quality narration. The interplay of offense and defense is fascinating, and the length of a frame, usually thirty to forty-five minutes, is a perfect time period for television. So why isn't this wonderful game more popular in the United States? For one thing, snooker tables aren't readily available. The game has its own equipment and terminology, and learning the detailed rules for fouls is a challenge. American players also love to pocket balls, which is much more difficult in

snooker. But the situation is changing. Now that many of the new billiard parlors opening across America are installing snooker tables, the game will surely have a loyal following in the United States before long.

Snooker uses a different table and smaller balls than billiards (opposite page). *Joe Johnson* (above) *takes a shot during the 1987 world snooker championship.*

3

TECHNIQUES

It's impossible to learn how to play pool just by reading a book, and this book offers no exception. Pool, like many sports and games, requires physical movements that are acquired by feel and experience and are difficult to describe in words. Most books on pool tell you what to shoot, rather than how to shoot. No book deals with such subtleties as when to raise the butt of your cue stick or how to draw the cue ball two lengths of the table.

The best a book can do is teach you how to learn. Here are four important points to remember if you want to be successful:

1. *Find a teacher.*

The best players are not necessarily the best teachers. Find someone who can *guide* you, not just beat you. A good instructor can watch you play for three minutes and correct ten flaws in your stance, bridge, and stroke, as well as prescribe exercises that will help you break bad habits.

2. *Study good players.*

Don't just watch them *play*, watch what they are *doing* as they play. It's very easy to get caught up as a spectator at a match and ignore the player's technique. You won't gain much from a pool player by looking at the object ball. Instead, observe the choice of shot and try to understand it. Then focus on the player's bridge and speed of stroke, noting what kind of english he is using and the extent of his follow-through. Only later should you look at the ball (after it is moving) to see what his intention was and how all of the other elements affected the shot.

3. *Practice.*

This doesn't mean spend six hours a day knocking the balls around. Unstructured practice is very injurious to your game, since you will only repeat errors (often without knowing it) and will not work on

Billiards can't be learned just by reading a book. A player such as David Leah (opposite page, playing snooker) owes his skills to practice, helpful teachers, and hours and hours of watching good players in action. A book can tell you what to shoot, but to really understand the subtleties of pool, you must apply yourself and let experience be your guide.

Maurice Vignaux (1846–1916) At six-foot-three and three hundred pounds Vignaux was an aristocratic and very dominating player. An ambidextrous champion, he won the world straight-rail title in 1875. He came in second in the first balkline tournament ever held in 1883. In 1903, a French court awarded him the 18.2 title after a dispute over how to resolve a tie among the three top players. In 1904, he took the world 18.1 title and held it until overthrown by Willie Hoppe in 1906. Vignaux was known as "The Old Lion" because of his flowing golden hair. His book *Le Billard*, written in 1889, is the most extensive volume ever published on carom technique.

correcting your weaknesses. During a given session, first devote time to practice, *then* have fun by playing a game or shooting for pleasure.

4. *Work on your attitude.*

Be receptive to new knowledge. You will see some hair-raising things happen on a billiard table—shots can be made in ways you never thought possible. You won't be able to duplicate them the first time, or maybe the first thousand times, but eventually you will understand what makes the balls behave the way they do.

Your mind can be your worst enemy in billiards. There are very few shots that are beyond your physical ability, so why can't you make them? It is largely a matter of psychology. While the motion of the cue stick is physical, your ability to control it is mental. If you are tired, ill, nervous, or insecure you will not be able to make the cue do your bidding. If noises or your opponent's habits bother you, your game will suffer, so try your best to shut out the world and focus totally on the green ocean and its colored spheres.

Every book on pool technique attempts to explain such fundamentals as stance, aiming, and stroke. Some even purport to tell you where to put your feet, where to hold the cue, and with how many fingers. But how do the authors know this when they've never even met you? If they don't know your age, height, weight, or strength, how good can their advice be? Many of these basic decisions depend on your physical measurements. In this sec-

tion I will show you how *you* can decide what kind of stance and stroke to use.

If you don't develop proper fundamentals, your game will suffer and you will likely never know why. It is possible, with practice, to learn to compensate for faulty technique, but why go through the extra effort? If you do things right at the outset, you will improve much more quickly. What is right? Each basic element is designed to accomplish a specific purpose. Once you know the objective, you will be able to adapt your posture and shoot at your best.

By no means do the following tips and bits of advice represent a complete discussion of these subjects. True beginners will need to consult one of the many books on basic playing technique and get at least a minimum amount of experience to be able to get the most out of this information.

Stance

The stance, your position while shooting, has two purposes: to keep your body stable while stroking, so that it doesn't interfere with the shot; and to permit the cue to swing freely. Balance is the most important component of stance. If you are out of balance, either your body will sway during the shot, or you will have to tense your muscles to prevent the motion. If your body shifts, unwanted movement will be transmitted to the cue ball. If your body is tense, you will not be able to control the cue ball and will become fatigued quickly.

Stroking requires the least effort when the forearm of your grip hand (the hand holding the butt end of the stick) is vertical just as you contact the ball; every other aspect of stance is dictated by this consideration. Now that you know what position the cue stick should be in as you hit the ball, it is your job to maneuver your body so that you are in balance at the time of contact. If you stand too far from the ball, you will have to lean over to hit it, which tends to make you fall forward during the stroke. If you stand too close, you won't be able to stroke freely.

The position of your head can vary greatly without affecting your stability. Some players barely bend over, which gives them an overview of the whole table. Others bend down almost to ball level and sight down the cue as if it were a rifle. While it is probably easier to judge english while bending over close to the ball, either position can be effective.

How far should you hold the cue stick away from your body? Willie Mosconi, fifteen-time world champion and the author of two books on technique, advocates keeping the grip arm as close to the body as possible without actually interfering with its ability to move freely. There are two reasons for this: (1) it is more difficult to achieve a straight pendulum motion with your arm stretched away from the body, and (2) it is easier to maintain a straight stroke because the torso helps confine the movement of the cue as you stroke.

Grip

The grip refers to the manner in which the butt end of the cue is held. (The manner of holding the tip end is called the "bridge.") A right-handed shooter grasps the butt in his right hand. Players differ in (1) where they hold the cue, (2) how many fingers they use to hold it, and (3) how much pressure they apply to the grip. Sources differ on exactly where the cue should be held. Charles C. Peterson, a tireless missionary of billiards, and exciting trick-shot player, always insisted that the cue should be held precisely at the balance point, because otherwise it would tend to dip forward or backward.

In fact, there is a range of acceptable grip points for each player that depends on height, stance, and arm span. A person with long arms will have to grip the cue farther back in order to make a free swing. Oliver Ortmann, a tall, young German player who won the 1989 U.S. Open Straight Pool Championship, holds the very end of the cue in a tight death grip when shooting; he had a run of 137 during the tournament. On the other hand, if you hold the cue too far back for your stance, you will have to lift the butt on your backswing, and you will be shooting down at the ball at the moment of contact. This will destroy your follow-through and will put unwanted backspin on your shots. Holding the cue too far forward will make it impossible for your forearm to be vertical when the ball is struck.

Most people grip the cue with either two or four fingers. The thumb is always used, along with either the forefinger or all others, except the pinkie (Ortmann uses all five fingers). The reason that a three-finger grip is not used is that it is difficult to make.

Bridge

The bridge is the arrangement of the fingers used to guide the shaft of the cue during stroking. The purpose of bridging is to provide support and direction for the cue stick as the ball is being struck. Failure to make a sound bridge dooms your game from the outset. Imagine holding a rifle with two fingers and shooting it at the same time.

The critical features of a bridge are (1) how the hand is supported by the table, (2) how the cue is guided by the fingers, and (3) the ease with which the height of the fingers can be varied in order to apply draw and follow.

Most books advocate a "closed-hand" bridge. But placing your fingers in this position can be painful if you are not used to it. If you can't make one, don't worry. Snooker requires the greatest aiming accuracy of all billiard games and all the top snooker players use open-hand bridges.

Forceful strokes require a closed bridge, however. The reason for this is that the cue stick actually bounces off the cue ball during contact and must be guided to complete the shot properly.

In a closed-hand bridge, the thumb,

index finger, and middle finger are used to guide the edge of the cue, and the larger the area of contact with the cue, the better. Since the fingers only constrain one side of the shaft, care must be taken not to sway the cue in the opposite direction during the stroke. Different bridges are used for different strokes. For a short nip, the cue can be held very firmly, since there will be little follow-through. A long, hard stroke requires a very stable but free bridge that will not resist the forward motion of the cue.

The most awkward bridge position occurs when you are trying to shoot over an object ball because there is no room on the table to form a conventional bridge. The key to this type of shot is to form some sort of groove in which to rest the cue, even if it is just a small one between the first joint of your thumb and the knuckle of your index finger. Since the cue will be elevated, controlling the stroke is very important. Even a small amount of english will make the ball curve. There is also a strong tendency to allow the tip to flip up just before contact and miss the ball entirely. (Note: If you don't actually make contact with any ball, you may try again without penalty.)

When you are close to a cushion, avoid the temptation to make an ordinary bridge on the rail. This will elevate the cue far too much for most shots. Instead, rest the shaft flat on the rail and form your fingers around it, using the middle finger as a guide.

Bridging is tough enough on most shots, but what happens if you can't even reach the cue ball? In these cases you can use the mechanical bridge—a piece of metal, wood, or plastic attached to a stick that is positioned on the table—to support the shaft of the cue. In Britain it is called, logically enough, a "rest."

The most common problems with a mechanical bridge are (1) keeping it steady during shooting, (2) guiding the cue in a straight line, and (3) the fact that the shaft can't be held tightly. When you form a bridge with your hand, you can feel the tension against your skin and gauge the amount of force needed. With a mechanical bridge, this information is absent.

Many players are unaware that it is acceptable to use more than one mechanical bridge for a shot. One can be stacked on top of another to create a higher bridge for shooting over balls.

European players dislike the mechanical bridge and will go to great lengths to avoid using it. Various long or pistonlike, extendable cues have been invented, as well as a sleeve that fits over the butt end of a cue to increase its length. But another alternative to the mechanical bridge for shots that are positioned inconveniently is to shoot with the opposite hand. Take fifteen to thirty minutes a day to practice this technique. Behind-the-back shooting is just silly—you can't even see what you are doing and have to contort yourself into an unbalanced stance.

After all this talk about bridges, you should know that some players use no bridge at all; they play one-handed, either

In snooker and billiards, the bridge, or arrangement of fingers used to guide the shaft of the cue, is crucial to a player's skill (opposite). The critical aspects of the bridge include: how the hand is supported by the table; how the cue is guided by the fingers; and how easily the height of the fingers can be adjusted.

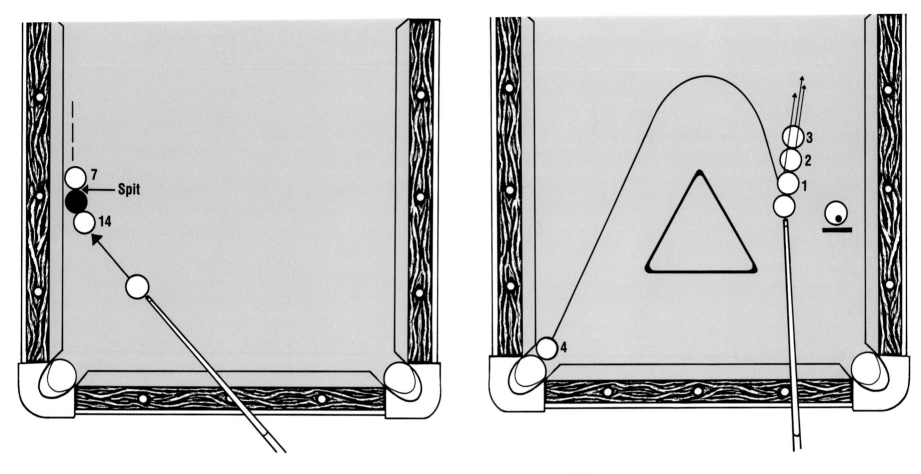

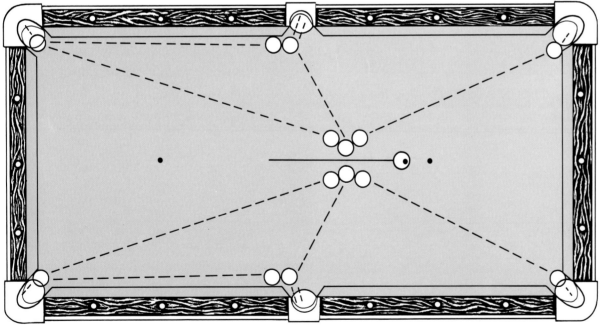

How it is possible to make fourteen balls in one stroke (left). Specialists at this type of shot have been able to sink over 25 balls at once. A saliva shot (above, left). Unless a small spot of saliva is applied at the point of contact of the two object balls, the seven-ball cannot be made in the corner pocket. Extreme draw is possible with an ordinary stroke if the cue ball is frozen to a line of object balls (above). The forward momentum of the stroke is imparted to the object balls, leaving the cue ball with tremendous backspin.

Artistic Billiards

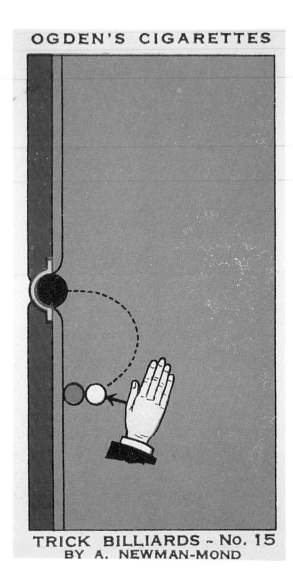

OGDEN'S CIGARETTES

TRICK BILLIARDS - No. 15
BY A. NEWMAN-MOND

Hand billiards. Extreme spin can be imparted by sliding the palm of the hand over the cue ball. Hand players were allowed to place the cue ball anywhere on the table prior to each shot. With this handicap they were the full equal of players who used a cue.

Fancy shots, particularly spectacular massés, have been the object of serious study and competition in Europe for over one hundred years. In the United States, fancy-shot matches have been held only rarely—the last was in 1931. The most dazzling shots, in terms of the path taken by the cue ball, form an entire discipline known as "artistic billiards," or "fantasy billiards." The competitive program consists of sixty-eight specific shots, revised from time to time by the sport's governing body, the Commission Internationale de Billard Artistique (CIBA). The balls are placed by the referee according to precise specifications and using a template, in some cases to a tolerance of a tenth of an inch. As in diving, each shot is assigned a degree of difficulty: a whole number between 4 and 11.

A player is given three opportunities to make each shot. If successful, the player is awarded a number of points equal to the degree of difficulty. The player scoring the greatest total is the winner. The program is organized to comprise a maximum of exactly 500 points. The largest total ever scored in competition was 355, by Raymond Steylaerts of Belgium in 1984. World competition began in 1936, but no tournament has ever been held in the United States. This is understandable, since not more than a handful of Americans can make a significant number of the shots.

CIBA rules specify that ivory balls must be used. Plastic balls produce too much friction with the cloth and render some of the difficult massé shots nearly impossible, since the spin wears off before the shot can be completed. Watching an artistic billiards exhibition is startling even for experienced pool players. If you ever have the opportunity to see one, don't miss it.

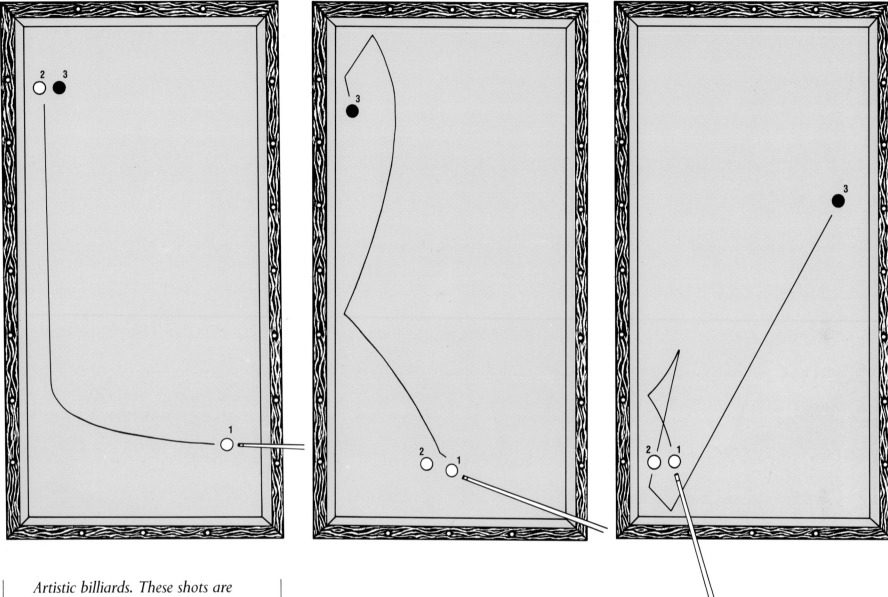

Artistic billiards. These shots are designed both to demonstrate the skill of the player and to amaze the audience. Many shots in the official program for artistic billiards are so difficult that only a handful of players in the United States can execute them. Most physicists will bet they are impossible, but they'll be wrong.

4

EQUIPMENT

Equipment is as important in billiards as in any other sport—you can't play well and enjoy the game with poor tools. To choose and evaluate equipment you need to understand its function as well as its construction. Once you do, you will be an informed purchaser of billiard paraphernalia. (Bear in mind at all times that good-looking equipment does not necessarily play well. A beautifully inlaid table may have cushions set at the wrong height; a flashy cue stick could warp after three months of use; and the fanciest brass light fixture may illuminate the table so poorly that your game will be affected.)

Tables

The table is the arena in which all the action in a pool game takes place, and its characteristics have a tremendous effect on play. The table has to be flat (smooth), level (so the balls will not drift due to gravity), and stable (so it won't move when people bump or lean against it). The cushions must produce a clean rebound, and the pockets must be sized and cut so that balls do not jump back out after entering. Satisfy these conditions, and you have a good table, no matter what it looks like cosmetically. But omit one of them, and you have a piece of junk.

The playing area of a billiard table, defined by the beveled edges of the cushions, is always exactly twice as long as it is wide. This was not always so. The rule in Charles Cotton's 1674 book required only that it be "somewhat longer than it is broad," but the 2:1 ratio was established by 1800.

How much space needs to be left clear around a billiard table depends on the circumstances. Any walls must be far enough away to permit a player to stand firmly and swing the cue fully. Some furniture can be moved, if necessary, to

Good equipment is very important in billiards. Once you understand how billiard equipment is made and how it works, you'll be able to determine what is the best equipment for you. The table (opposite) is from Blatt Billiards, of New York City.

A good billiard equipment store should offer a variety of tables. These four tables are from Blatt Billiards, of New York City.

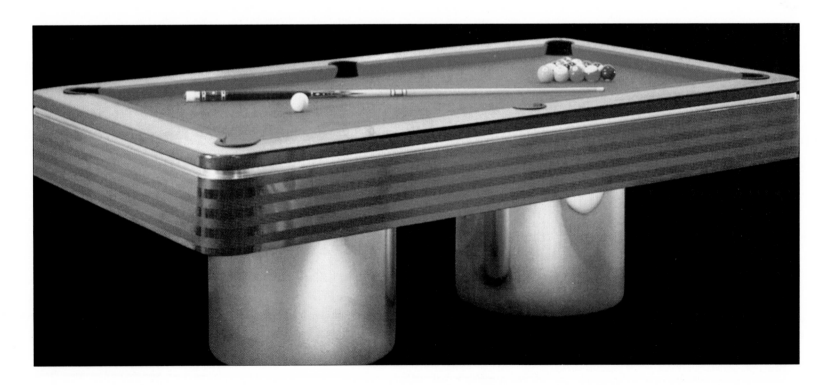

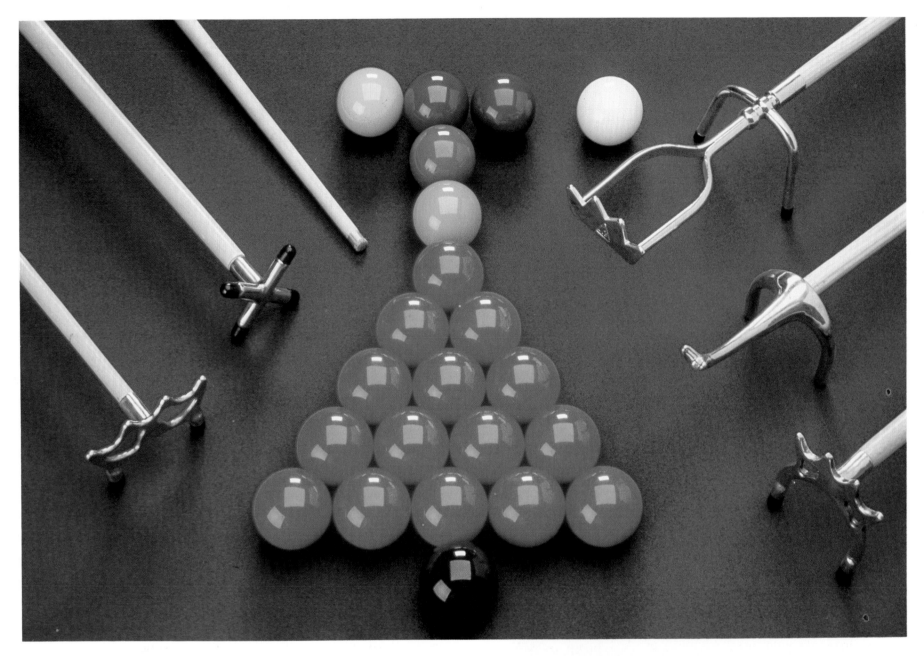

These photos show why snooker is such a difficult game. The balls are small, cue tips are small, and the pockets seem microscopic. As if that weren't enough, the table is so large you need to use a bridge much more often.

Chalk

Two types of chalk are used in billiards: cue chalk and hand chalk. The function of cue chalk is to increase the friction between the cue tip and the cue ball to prevent miscues. An unchalked leather tip is quite slippery and can only be used to hit the cue ball near its center. If you don't believe chalk is important, try an experiment. Wipe all of the chalk off your tip with a cloth. Now shoot at an object ball located one foot away from the cue ball with heavy right english. It's a safe bet the cue ball won't even hit the object ball! After this test you will probably develop the correct habit of chalking before every shot.

The objective in applying chalk is to coat the tip with a thin but even layer. In order to do this, you must look at the tip after you apply chalk to ensure that there are no uncovered areas. Too many players grab the chalk, squeak it against the tip a few times, and assume they have done an adequate job. After miscuing, they look at the tip, puzzled, and shake their heads.

A thick layer of chalk will actually begin to *reduce* friction with the ball. If you find you have put on too much chalk, wipe it off with a cloth or tissue. Do not blow it off the tip, as this will add a layer of moisture. Also, don't wipe the chalk off with your finger, since this mixes oil from your skin with the chalk.

Cue chalk is not actually made of chalk (calcium carbonate), but is an abrasive powder and colorant suspended in a fixative to give the cube a conveniently hard form. The fact that the material is abrasive means that continued use will eventually wear away the tip. Care should be taken to prevent the chalk material from rubbing against the ferrule, to which the tip is attached. Constant grinding will wear it away as well, and a ferrule is much more difficult to replace than a tip. Do not chalk the cue over the table. Excess chalk will immediately fall on the cloth, where the balls will pick it up.

Hand chalk, usually talcum powder, is used to dry the hands and *reduce* the friction between the bridge hand and the shaft of the cue. Many people use too much, and it gets on the cloth and the balls. If your hands are sticky it is better to go wash and dry them thoroughly. If you really need chalk, get a hard cone of chalk that you can rub your finger over to deposit a thin layer only where needed.

Women were not permitted to use cues for more than a hundred years after they first appeared, out of fear that they might tear the cloth with a pointed instrument. This precaution was set aside after the tip was invented in the early years of the nineteenth century. The woman here is applying white chalk to the tip of her cue. The table is extremely unusual in that the cushions are scalloped. This etching is from about 1850; no known examples of this table style have survived.

Balls

The first billiard balls were made of wood, a terrible material from a playing standpoint, but very easy to shape. After experiments with other materials, including stone, ivory was settled on by the year 1627. It is fine in many respects, but not all. Ivory balls are costly and difficult to keep round. They are also severely affected by temperature changes and can shatter without warning when suddenly exposed to cold.

You will almost never see ivory balls. Concerns for diminishing elephant populations have led to widespread bans on the importation of ivory. If you run across an old set in an antiques shop, there is little chance that they can be restored to playing condition. Ivory balls have always been expensive because one elephant tusk yields only three or four balls. For this reason, the search for an ivory substitute began in the middle of the nineteenth century and was the motivation behind John Wesley Hyatt's invention of celluloid in 1868. For the past hundred years, a vast number of materials have been tried. The finest balls are made of impact-resistant plastic by the German firm Raschig, though Brunswick has recently resumed manufacturing its famed Centennial ball.

Balls differ in density, size, weight, and resiliency. These factors, in turn, influence the speed of the balls and the angle at which they rebound from one another and the cushions. International carom balls are 61.5 millimeters (2.4 inches) in diameter and have a lot of inertia, which means they are much more difficult to spin than pocket billiard balls, which can weigh forty percent less.

Balls were first stained for color in the 1770s. The need for multiple colors was made necessary by English pool in the

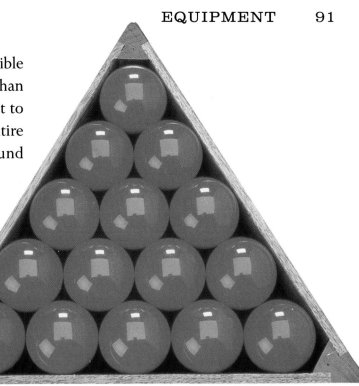

nineteenth century, in which each player required a distinct ball. Later, numbers were engraved on the balls. The present coloring scheme of several hues repeated on solid and striped balls—in the order of yellow, blue, red, purple, orange, green, and maroon—is about one hundred years old.

It is said that the earth is relatively smoother than a billiard ball. Here is what that means: A ball is permitted to vary by .005 inches out of a typical diameter of 2.25 inches, which is about 1 part in 500. The greatest depth in the ocean and the height of the tallest peak on earth are both around 30,000 feet, which calculated with a diameter of 8,000 miles amounts to about 1 part in 750, much less significant than the variance on a billiard ball.

The action of balls is strongly affected by dust, chalk, and grease on their surface. Balls should be cleaned before each use. At times it may even be necessary to wipe off the cue ball while playing.

Lighting

Effective lighting is often overlooked when setting up a billiard room. It is sometimes even ignored in favor of an attractive fixture. The objective is to focus attention on the balls and table without causing eye fatigue after hours of play. There should be no peripheral distrac-

tions, and the balls should cast no visible shadow. Incandescent light is better than fluorescent, but it is extremely difficult to produce even illumination over the entire table surface using individual round bulbs.

The degree to which varying light levels affects play goes unnoticed by most players. International rules permit the luminance to vary only by about fourteen percent over the entire surface of the table, a standard almost never achieved in the United States. Try this experiment. Go into your local poolroom with a photographer's light meter. Lay the meter on top of a piece of paper, with its aperture facing straight up. Starting in one corner of the table, slowly pull the paper on a diagonal to the opposite corner, and observe how the light level changes. It should read 560 lux (about 52 footcandles) everywhere—but it won't. You may be shocked to see how poorly the corners are illuminated. If the light fixture consists of three incandescent lights, the middle bulb should be a *lower* wattage than the outer two, or there will be a "hot spot" in the center of the table. For fixtures located forty inches above the cloth (a good average height), use 150-watt bulbs on the outside and a 100-watt bulb in between.

Choosing A Pool Hall

Irving Crane (1913–) "The Deacon" learned pocket billiards the right way—as a student of Jerome Keogh, the inventor of straight pool. He began at age eleven, ran 89 at age fourteen, and won the Rochester, New York, city tournament at fifteen. He began world-title competition in 1937, won in 1942, and went on to earn it five more times, the last in 1972.

Crane earned the pool-longevity record by entering world-title events during five different decades, from 1937 until 1974. A car salesman by occupation, Crane is a deadly accurate shooter whose favorite domain is the larger, five-by-ten-foot table. He has appeared in several film shorts and has written two introductory books on the subject. Also a world-class three-cushion player, Crane's best performance in the World Tournament was a sixth-place finish in 1952.

When most localities supported at most one billiard parlor, it was not difficult to decide where to play. However, as of April 1990, New York had almost fifty licensed rooms, with a new one appearing every other week or so. Establishments are opening all across the country, and soon most cities will offer a choice of poolrooms. By being a knowledgeable consumer of billiard services, you can exert direct influence on the quality of specific rooms and even affect their survival.

Just as a bar can be crowded even though it serves bad drinks, pool halls can be jammed despite offering poor equipment and an environment that is not conducive to serious play. If you are going out to knock the balls around, meet people, or listen to loud music, you are after entertainment and will pick your spot on that basis. There's nothing wrong with shooting a little pool while hanging out—have fun! If you are interested in learning the game and improving your skills, you need a different sort of place. First, check out the general atmosphere. Be sure that there is adequate ventilation, so you won't be playing in a cloud of cigarette smoke. Loud music will also upset your concentration. Soft music can help your game, since it obscures other conversations and can be relaxing, but loud rock can make you miscue.

Next, see who's playing in the room. If there are no good players around, you won't learn anything there, and you ought to wonder why the good players are playing somewhere else.

Take note of the physical layout. Is there enough room between tables, or will you spend your time waiting for players at neighboring tables to shoot? If the tables are fewer than six feet apart, make a beeline for the exit. Also, be sure there are no pillars in inconvenient places.

Is there a carom table in the room? How about snooker tables? If you only see pool tables, and the room has more than twenty of them, you can assume that the owner is interested only in quick profits and doesn't care about the business' long-term prospects. If you were to ask why there aren't any billiard tables, you might be told that there aren't enough players. But of course there will never be enough billiard players if there is no table for them to learn and play on.

Study the equipment next. Take a look at the cloths on the tables. Are there tears or worn spots? Look closely at the spot where the balls are racked. Can you see dimples or lighter areas? Are there telltale lines in the cloth from the head of the table to the foot spot from break shots? If you can see them, the cloth should have been changed weeks or months ago.

Are the tops of the rails clean, or are they burned from cigarettes? Are the rails

Pool for Drinks, *a wood
engraving by W. A. Rogers in
Harper's Weekly, July 30, 1881.
The sight of minors in pool halls
led to a crackdown by politicians
and law-enforcement officials.*

Most people today want nothing to do with hustling (though it might excite them to know it is going on). In an effort to keep hustlers away from civilians, many new poolrooms forbid loitering near the tables. This policy permits people to play for money by agreement, but keeps vultures away from players who don't want to be accosted. It remains to be seen how long the prohibition can be maintained. When rooms are crowded, nobody wants hustlers around—they're more trouble than they're worth. But when business falls off, they provide a steady income. Once the hustlers take over a room, however, legitimate customers will not be seen again.

Even if you recognize that Eddie is a hustler, you can still be taken in by a variety of proposition bets that seem too generous to refuse. Many a victim has spent years trying to figure out why he lost. Here are two such bets, with explanations provided, in case you might be tempted.

Fifty against two in the side. It's simple. You and Eddie are going to play straight pool. When he gets to 50 points, he wins. All you have to do is sink *two balls* in the side pockets before he reaches 50. (He can use all the pockets, but you only keep shooting if you pocket a ball in either side.) How can you lose? After all, Eddie might be better, but he's not *twenty-five times* better. Even if he plays you safe all the time, surely you'll be able to bank in a couple of balls. You can drop hundreds at this game and still think you had a chance. Here is what will happen. If you

Guess I'll go and fight the Germans too.

British postcard, c. 1915. Billiards has long been popular with the military, and has often been used in propaganda materials.

Steve Mizerak (1944–) Known the world over for his Miller Beer commercials, Mizerak started playing pool at age four, learning the game from his father, who held the New Jersey pocket billiard title several times during the 1950s. Young Steve had run 50 by age eleven and 100 by age thirteen. A student of Mosconi, he won the United States open straight pool title four consecutive times, from 1970 to 1973. He took the world straight pool title in 1982 and 1983. At the time of his induction into the BCA Hall of Fame he was the youngest player ever elected.

Nick Varner (1948–) Varner is one of the few National Collegiate Pool champions to make a successful transition to the ranks of the professional. He took the world straight pool title with wins in the PPPA Open in 1980 and 1986. In 1980 he also won the BCA National Eight-Ball championship. In 1989, he dominated nine-ball competition with eight major victories, and was named *Billiards Digest* Player of the Year for the second time. A mild-mannered and friendly Kentuckian, Varner is a room owner, cue manufacturer, and exhibition player. His induction into the Hall of Fame came in 1990.

break, you're already in trouble, so assume Eddie breaks. He will hit the apex ball with a little draw, spreading the pack nicely and leaving the cue ball near the center of the table. All the object balls will lie below the foot spot, so you won't even have a bank shot or even be able to make a good safety. Every time he comes to the table, Eddie will first clear away any balls you could possibly make in a side pocket. If he thinks he might miss, he will play safe by leaving the cue ball very close to a side pocket. Even if you manage to bank one in from a crazy angle, you probably won't have another shot. You might even scratch, in which case your ball comes back up and now you have to make *three* in the side to win. It's amazing how fast Eddie will get to 50. Between equal players (and remember, you're not his equal), a fair game might be 50 against one in the side.

One-ball nine-ball. OK, the last gambit was too lopsided. Here's one in which it looks like Eddie doesn't have a chance. The game is ordinary nine-ball, with standard rules, but if you legally sink any *one* of the balls numbered two through nine, you win. Eddie has to sink the one ball to win, and *he* has to break! If *you* sink it, he can't win. The way the sucker views this game, he has eight chances at cash, while Eddie only has one. But the only way you will ever take one of these racks is if Eddie lets you. First of all, he isn't going to play a standard break shot, but will try a special one that is designed to send the one ball into a side pocket. There is a good chance (better than 1 in

Wood engraving from the National Police Gazette, *December 14, 1885. While women did frequent pool halls, they weren't always there to shoot pool. The* Police Gazette *was the* National Enquirer *of its day.*

3) that he will win on the first shot. If he doesn't, consider what you are facing. Now in order to win, you have to sink the one *and another ball*. Eddie only has to pocket the one, and he's a better player than you are! Your eight-to-one advantage didn't just disappear; it was never there at all.

At least in a proposition game, you theoretically have a chance to shoot. And, after all, you might get lucky and win. But there's an altogether different class of hustle, the "impossible" trick shot. In this one, you don't even get to touch the cue! Eddie sets up a shot that defies your intuition and the laws of physics. You figure that even God would have a tough time making it, so a twenty-dollar wager seems like peanuts. Eddie steps up to the table and—bang!—the ball and your money disappear in a flash. Your chances would be better at three-card monte. For a perfect vignette demonstrating this ruse, watch the opening scene of *The Hustler*, before the opening title even appears. There is very little on a billiard table that is really impossible.

If you hang around a poolroom long enough, you will see everything and, if history can be relied upon, you will probably bet against it and lose your money. Unshaven men will offer to play you left-handed, one-handed, or even no-handed (using their feet). They may propose to push the ball with their hands, nose, or mouth or with such unorthodox instruments as brooms or umbrellas. Avoid them. They're not kidding—they can do everything they say. Let them sucker

someone else while you sit back and enjoy the show.

Don't imagine that hustling is confined to men. Males will do well to suppress any sexist notion they may have that they can always beat a woman. It is far more likely you will be led into giving *her* a spot when *you* should be receiving one. In short, when your female opponent wants to play a little "money ball," run for the exit.

However low a hustler may be, it gets worse when he cheats. It is embarrassing to report that the catalog of treachery in pool is long indeed. Without offering explicit instruction in such techniques, here are some nefarious examples. One of the easiest tricks is to keep the score incorrectly, called "rubbing the wire," after the wire where the score beads are strung. When the hustler scores 12 points, he marks up 13. If you catch him, he quickly apologizes for his "mistake." Gaffing the equipment is harder to detect. In eight-ball, the hustler may rub some polish on the striped balls before the game begins. This will have a significant effect on the angle at which they will rebound from the cue ball. It doesn't matter whether you wind up with the stripes or the solids; if Eddie is stuck with polished ones, he will know how to compensate. You won't.

Chalk or a touch of saliva can be applied to a ball at a key point in the game. Moistening the chalk cube will make it difficult for you to chalk the tip and will increase your chance of a mis-cue. Misracking is also fertile ground for

Mike Sigel (1953–) "Captain Hook" began playing pool at thirteen and turned professional at twenty. He took the United States open nine-ball title in 1975 through 1977 and again in 1982; the world eight-ball title in 1976; first place in the world one-pocket competition in 1978, and the world straight pool championship in 1979, 1981, and 1985. His stroke is so powerful that he occasionally shatters a cue stick on a nine-ball break shot. In 1987, Sigel became the first pool professional to earn over one-hundred-thousand dollars in prize money in a single year. He is the youngest male to have been elected to the BCA Hall of Fame.

Billiards played on a bicycle (left).
*Prints exist showing the game
being played on horseback* (above),
*aboard ship, in a dirigible, and on
double-decker buses.*

chicanery. It is a universal custom for a player to rack for his opponent. By failing to freeze the balls or tilting the rack slightly, Eddie can make a joke of your break shot.

How do you beat a hustler? Even if you are a better player, you won't necessarily win. Eddie will persuade you to give him a handicap large enough to eliminate your advantage. If you are weaker, he won't give you an adequate spot. The balance doesn't depend on your relative skills as players, but on your ability at deception. All of his calculations are based on what he thinks he knows about your game and what he thinks you know about his. If you feed him disinformation, you might have a chance. Of course, this advice reduces you to his level and the contest then becomes a battle between two thieves. Suppose you refuse to conceal your true speed. Can you still win? In general, no. You have to be playing against a hustler who lets his mark win some games at the outset. If you are ahead and he wants to raise the stake, quit. If *he* wins a game, again, quit. If he offers a better handicap and wants a chance to win his money back, just smile and say, "Are you a hustler, Eddie?"

Allen Gilbert (1929–) Gilbert, one of the few important players to use a slip stroke (in which the cue stick is actually thrown at rather than pushed through the cue ball), is the strongest American three-cushion player since the 1950s. He won the national championship in 1968, 1970, 1971, 1977, and 1988 and represented the United States in the world tournament in 1968 to 1971, 1977 to 1979, and 1984 to 1986. His book, *Systematic Billiards* (1977), explains diamond systems never before described in print. An intense student of billiard technique and equipment, particularly cue sticks, Gilbert is now one of the permanent players in the Billiard World Cup Association professional tour.

Possibly the best advice on how to handle a shark was offered by Charles Cotton in *The Compleat Gamester* in 1674:

To conclude, let me advise you, if you play let not a covetous desire of winning another's money engage you to the losing of your own; which will not only disturb your mind, but by the disreputation of being a Gamester, if you lose not your estate, you will certainly lose your credit, and good name, than which there is nothing more valuable.

6

TOURNAMENTS

While billiards by its nature is a battle between two players, the idea of inviting the audience to watch is relatively recent. The first public billiard match for a money stake was played in Syracuse, New York, in May 1854, when Joseph White beat George Smith at the American four-ball game for a two-hundred-dollar purse. The idea of actually charging the spectators for admission began in 1859 with a historic two-day series in Detroit. The final stake was fifteen thousand dollars, an astronomical sum in the years before the Civil War. Each spectator had paid five dollars for admission, unheard of in a time when a theatre ticket went for ten cents, and hundreds had to be turned away at the door.

Triangular tournaments, consisting of three players, were popular in the 1860s, while the first world tournament at billiards (straight-rail, although it was called French caroms at the time) was held in New York in 1873 and won by Albert Garnier, a wealthy Frenchman. From that time until the late 1940s, championship titles changed hands either through tournaments or challenge matches. Tournaments in the nineteenth century were well-attended but complex affairs. Each player was permitted to be represented by a second (as in a duel of pistols), who was also called an umpire. The duty of the umpire was to look out for the interests of his player. He would inspect the equipment, negotiate special rules, call fouls and make sure that the opponent gained no undue advantage from the proceedings. Immediately before a match, the two umpires would select an impartial referee, who was usually a famous player not participating in the tournament. This choice often took a long time, as each umpire had veto power and there was no one to break deadlocks. Even if they agreed on a choice, there was no guarantee that the individual selected would

Tournaments have come a long way since the first public billiard match for a money stake was played in Syracuse, New York, in 1854. The Hofmeister World Doubles Snooker Championship in Northampton, England, (opposite) drew a captive audience in 1984.

The scene at the first match for the championship of America (right), won by Michael Phelan, on April 11, 1859. His first prize of $15,000 is only rarely equalled in pool tournaments today.

At left is Billiard player, Dudley Kavanagh.

consent, and even if he did, there was always the possibility he might quit in the middle of a match if he found the taunts of the crowd too unnerving. This was a day in which the audience was an active participant in the game, loudly expressing its views and emotions with a chorus of yelling and banging of feet (recall that many of the audience members had a financial interest in the outcome). The audience even had an official role—if the referee failed to see something (such as a shot or an alleged foul), he was allowed to ask the spectators for their opinion!

The referee was charged with some unusual duties. During the last half of the nineteenth century, tables were illuminated by open gas jets. After Thomas Wallace burned his hand severely while attempting a massé shot near the center of the table, a rule was added permitting the referee to hold the gas fixture aside for the player while he was shooting.

During the early decades of the twentieth century, championship titles in both pool and billiards changed hands through challenge matches. The titleholder had to consent to play challengers, sometimes as often as six times per year. If the challenger won, he became the new champion. Matches under this system were intimate and intense; with only two contestants, the audience could focus on the game.

Players found the stress of challenge matches to be tremendous, since a single error in a game could mean loss of a title. During the 1920s, challenges were replaced by multiplayer tournaments. They took longer to play, but the loss of a single game could be offset by winning other games.

Modern Tournaments

A tournament should be organized to accomplish several objectives. First, it should offer a fair method of ranking the players, and it must do this in a way that is entertaining for spectators and not unduly tiring for the players. This limits the total number of games that can be played, the length of the competition, and the number of matches that any player is compelled to play in one day. If more than one table is being used, some effort should be made to rotate play so that no one has an advantage from using the same table repeatedly. Similarly, no player should be forced to play too many games early in the morning or late at night (and certainly not an early match right after a late-night duel). Add to all this the need to maintain audience interest by keeping the final result in doubt until the last round, and you can see that organizing a successful tournament is a real challenge.

Top players are usually "seeded" throughout the field of players in such a way that they will not face one another in preliminary games. This tends to guarantee that the final matches will be competitive. Another practice used to protect top-ranking players is to give them "byes," or allow them to sit out the opening rounds. This increases the chances that they will survive to the finals.

Raymond Ceulemans (1937–) The Belgian Ceulemans (pronounced "Kool-a-muns") is the most outstanding carom player of the twentieth century, rivalling Hoppe in all respects. An amiable, heavy-set player, he has been called "Mr. 100" since winning his one-hundredth major tournament. He has been world champion at three-cushions, cushion caroms, straight-rail, 47.1 balkline, and a combination event of five carom games known as "pentathlon." He totally dominated three-cushion play from 1963 through 1985, setting new records for high run and average. Ceulemans is also an accomplished artistic billiards player.

In England, snooker tournaments are a popular spectator sport, and the arenas are elaborate.

Throughout the history of billiard competition, only three types of tournaments have ever been popular: *round-robin, single elimination* and *double elimination*. In a round-robin, everyone plays everyone else at least once, possibly several times. In a double-round-robin event, for example, every pair of players meets twice.

The round-robin format is considered the most fair, since no one can claim that his schedule was easier or harder than anyone else's. One significant drawback, though, is that a large number of games have to be played. If there are *n* number of players, then $n(n-1)/2$ games are needed. For 32 players, a single round-robin requires 496 games, probably an unacceptably long ordeal for both competitors and gallery. For a smaller field, however, say eight players, a round-robin system works well. It also ensures that the weaker players will have a chance to meet the stronger ones, and there is always the possibility of a "spoiler," when an unranked contestant unexpectedly beats a favorite.

A second problem with a round-robin tournament is that several players may finish with tied records, requiring laborious playoffs. In some instances tournaments have ended with *all* the players tied, a total disaster for everyone who is involved.

One last difficulty has not been resolved by any known tournament method in any sport. Suppose that player A wins with a record of 9–1, his one loss being to player B, who had a record of 8–2. While we have no hesitation in declaring

A the best competitor overall, it seems difficult to say that he is superior to B, who beat him! As we shall see, the elimination format doesn't cure this trouble either.

A single-elimination event combines players in the treelike structure used in tennis tournaments. Once a player loses, he is out of contention, while winners move on to subsequent rounds. The overall winner is the one player who remains undefeated at the end. Single-elimination tournaments require the smallest number of games—if there are *n* players, only $n-1$ matches need be played—and no ties are possible for first or second place. But this method is seldom used in pool, because it is very risky even for good players. The possibility of an unlucky early loss (resulting in elimination) makes people reluctant to enter, especially if an entry fee, travel expenses, and accommodations are required. Weak players don't want to enter since they're sure they will be beaten, and thus have no chance to win.

A compromise is the double-elimination format, usually arranged in a "split-double" structure. A player must lose two games to be out, which means that no one can be eliminated by one bad game. In effect, two single-elimination trees are played simultaneously. First-round losers enter the "losers' bracket," while winners remain in the "winners' bracket." Losers from later rounds of the winners' bracket remain alive by reappearing in the losers' bracket. Losers from the losers' bracket have lost twice

Ewa Mataya (1964–) Mataya was a model in Sweden before entering professional pool, taking the championship of her native land in 1981. Winner of the United States open title in 1988, she set a new straight-pool high-run mark with a 54 the following year.

Mataya also won the United States open nine-ball title in 1988. An enthusiastic student of the game and its history, she provides insightful commentary for ESPN pool events and gives exhibitions for Brunswick Corporation.